D0573906

Endpapers:
Cavalry Charge on the Southern Plains,
detail, by Frederic Remington, 1907, oil,
The Metropolitan Museum of Art,
Gift of Several Gentlemen, 1911

THE ART OF THE OLD WEST

by SHIRLEY GLUBOK

Designed by Gerard Nook

The Macmillan Company, New York, New York
Collier-Macmillan Ltd., London

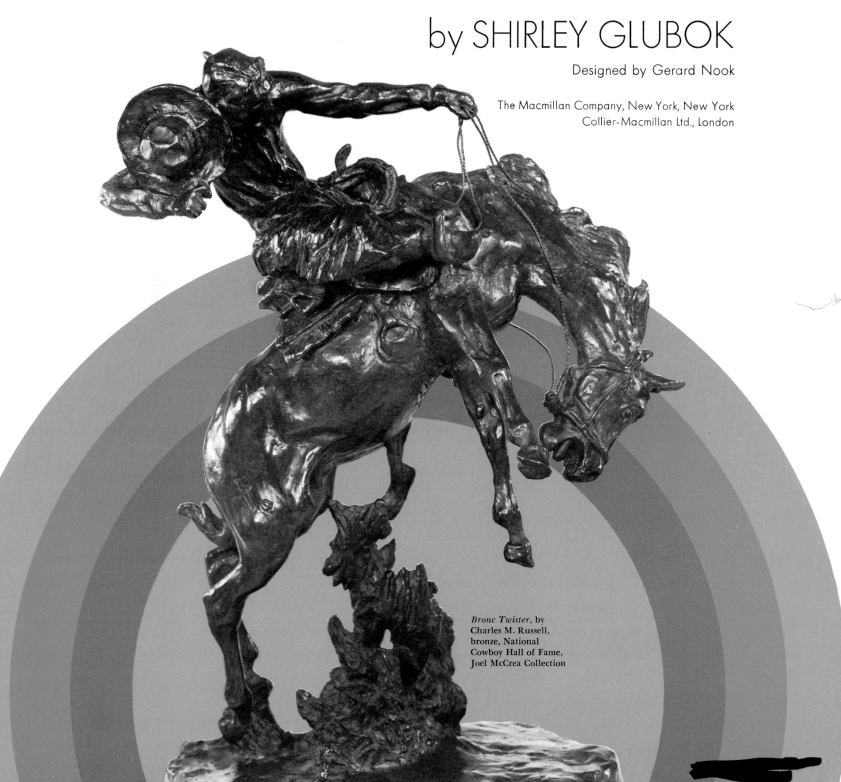

Bronc Twister, by Charles M. Russell, bronze, National Cowboy Hall of Fame, Joel McCrea Collection

The author gratefully acknowledges the assistance of: *Robert A. Ewing,* Curator-in-charge of Fine Arts, Museum of New Mexico; *Opal M. Harber,* Librarian III, Western History Department, Denver Public Library; *Peter H. Hassrick,* Curator of Collections, Amon Carter Museum; *John K. Howat,* Curator of American Painting and Sculpture, The Metropolitan Museum of Art; *William R. Johnston,* Assistant Director, The Walters Art Gallery; *Coy L. Ludwig,* Former Director, Remington Art Museum; *William E. Marshall,* Director, State Historical Society of Colorado; *Weston J. Naef,* Assistant Curator, Department of Prints and Photographs, The Metropolitan Museum of Art; *Natalie Spassky,* Curatorial Assistant, American Painting and Sculpture, The Metropolitan Museum of Art; *Eve Sicular* and *Mark Oshima;* and especially the helpful cooperation of *John C. Ewers,* Senior Ethnologist, Smithsonian Institution, and *Stuart P. Feld.*

Other books by Shirley Glubok:

THE ART OF ANCIENT EGYPT

THE ART OF LANDS IN THE BIBLE

THE ART OF ANCIENT GREECE

THE ART OF THE NORTH AMERICAN INDIAN

THE ART OF THE ESKIMO

THE ART OF ANCIENT ROME

THE ART OF AFRICA

ART AND ARCHAEOLOGY

THE ART OF ANCIENT PERU

THE ART OF THE ETRUSCANS

THE ART OF ANCIENT MEXICO

KNIGHTS IN ARMOR

THE ART OF INDIA

THE ART OF JAPAN

THE ART OF COLONIAL AMERICA

THE ART OF THE SOUTHWEST INDIANS

THE FALL OF THE AZTECS

THE FALL OF THE INCAS

DISCOVERING TUT-ANKH-AMEN'S TOMB

DISCOVERING THE ROYAL TOMBS AT UR

DIGGING IN ASSYRIA

HOME AND CHILD LIFE IN COLONIAL DAYS

Cover illustration: *The Bravado,* detail, by Alfred Jacob Miller, after 1837, watercolor, The Walters Art Gallery, Baltimore. Photograph by Alfred Tamarin

Copyright © 1971 Shirley Glubok. All rights reserved. No part of this book may be reproduced or transmitted in any form or by any means, electronic or mechanical, including photocopying, recording or by any information storage and retrieval system, without permission in writing from the publisher. The Macmillan Company, 866 Third Avenue, New York, N.Y. 10022. Collier-Macmillan Canada Ltd., Toronto, Ontario. Library of Congress catalog card number: 79-123138. Printed in the United States of America.

1 2 3 4 5 6 7 8 9 10

1.73
G44

1820, watercolor, American Philosophical Society

The United States was a very young country when Americans began exploring the vast lands west of the Mississippi River. The first expeditions crossed into the West in the early 1800's. With them went pioneer artists who brought back sketches of the Indian people, the scenery and the wildlife.

One of the earliest pioneer artists was Titian R. Peale, who went west at nineteen. He was the first American to make drawings of the buffalo, the prairie chicken, the black-tailed deer, above, and other animals native to the West.

Peale's father, artist Charles Willson Peale, founded the first American museum, in Philadelphia. Peale's Museum exhibited the earliest portraits of Western Indians.

1832, oil,
Smithsonian
Institution

A self-taught painter named George Catlin admired the Indian portraits in Peale's Museum. Then one day he saw a group of Western Indians on their way to Washington. Catlin decided to paint the Indians in their home lands before settlers reached them and changed their ways.

In 1832 he traveled up the Missouri River on the first steamboat to make the trip. He went into Indian villages and painted portraits of the chiefs and other members of the tribes.

At right is Man-Mah-To-He-Ha, known as Old Bear, a medicine man of the Mandan Indians. He wears a bearskin around his waist and fox tails attached to his heels. In each hand he holds a ceremonial pipestem,

1832, oil, Smithsonian Institution

decorated with eagle feathers. His headdress and face paint are different from that of Chief Tchan-Dee, at left, known as Tobacco, of the Oglala Sioux Indians.

1832, oil,
Smithsonian
Institution

At left is Catlin's portrait of Kee-o-Kuk, known as The Running Fox, chief of the Sauk and Foxes. The proud, dignified chief is shown with a tomahawk, a war shield, a lance and a necklace of grizzly-bear claws.

Before Catlin's visit the Indians had never seen lifelike portraits. At first they were afraid to have their portraits painted. They feared that the painter was a medicine man who would take away some of their power if he made likenesses of them.

Catlin exhibited his gallery of Indian portraits in American cities and in Europe. The European exhibits often included live demonstrations by Indians of tribal dancing and singing.

Early paintings of the interiors of Indian homes were made by Peter Rindisbacher, who came from Switzerland to settle in the Red River Valley. In the cozy family scene at right, Indians are gathered around a fire on the floor of the lodge.

Indian Women in Tent, about 1833, watercolor, The West Point Museum Collections, U.S. Military Academy

arl Bodmer, a Swiss artist, journeyed up the Missouri River a year after Catlin, on the same steamboat. Bodmer was traveling with Prince Maximilian, a German scholar who was making scientific observations and writing a book.

The illustration below shows the Buffalo Dance of the Mandans, part of a ceremony to bring back the wandering buffalo herds. The Mandan dancers carried weapons and wore buffalo masks to represent both the hunters and the buffalo. The artist has caught the excitement of the human figures in action.

Bodmer was the first artist to visit the Blackfoot Indian country. In the illustration at right, a splendid Blackfoot rides off to war.

1843 engraving from an 1834
drawing, Smithsonian Institution

Huge herds of buffalo, numbering many millions, roamed the Western

Plains. In this buffalo hunting scene by an unknown artist, the feeling of speed

and action is given by the flowing hair of the hunter and his horse.

The painting was derived from an earlier work by Catlin.

Buffalo Hunter, after 1840, oil,
The Santa Barbara Museum of Art, Buell Hammett Memorial Fund

Landing the Charettes, after 1837, The Walters Art Gallery

Alfred Jacob Miller was one of the first artists to make sketches of the overland

route to the Far West that was later known as the Oregon Trail. He joined a

wagon train transporting supplies for fur trappers and goods to trade with the

Indians. As the caravan advanced, Miller made rapid drawings of the wagons,

horses and drivers, as well as of fur traders and Indians he encountered along the way.

Above is Miller's watercolor of the wagon train fording a river and climbing up

a steep bank. The horses and mules are straining to drag their heavy loads.

Beating a Retreat, detail, after 1837, oil,
Museum of Fine Arts, Boston, M. and M. Karolik Collection

When Miller painted Indians he was interested in showing action rather than individual character and details of costume. In a journal of his adventures, the artist described the painting above as a "Sioux raider being driven off by the Blackfeet." However, it is unlikely that Miller actually witnessed such a battle between Indian tribes.

Miller painted the hard, lonely lives of the fur trappers, the mountain men who had reached the Rockies long before the West was settled. Below, a handsome young trapper is taking a beautiful Indian girl as his bride. The bride's father stands behind her, presenting her to her new husband, as the chief and a friend of the groom look on. In the background is a gathering of Indian people, including a papoose in its cradle board.

Trapper's Bride,
after 1837, watercolor,
The Walters Art Gallery

Chippewa Indians Playing Checkers, about 1848, oil, Collection of Ambassador and Mrs. J. William Middendorf II, photograph courtesy of Hirschl and Adler Galleries

Captain Seth Eastman was a professional army officer as well as a painter who was deeply interested in the Indians. Stationed on the Western frontier for many years, he made studies of Indian people. Many of these Indians were beginning to take on the ways of the white man.

Eastman's painting above shows a scene in Minnesota. Two Chippewas are playing a game of checkers while a third watches.

Captain Eastman was invited by a committee of the House of Representatives to paint Indian scenes for the Capitol in Washington, D.C. The painting of women gathering wild rice is one of this series.

Eastman also produced 275 pages of drawings to illustrate a six-volume publication about the habits and customs of the Indians.

Rice Gatherers, late 1860's, oil,
United States Capitol Collection

Cowboys Roping a Bear, 1877,
oil, The Denver Art Museum

Spanish cowboys, or vaqueros, were painted by James Walker, who spent many

years in Mexico and California. The Spaniards brought the first horses and

cattle to the New World and introduced the customs of herding cattle on horseback,

the round-up and branding livestock.

In this painting, California cowboys are engaged in bearbaiting, the cruel

practice of tormenting bears. They are dressed in typical vaquero clothes: vests

and chaps studded with silver buttons and flat-topped hats, or sombreros.

Early Canadian Indian life has been preserved by the artist Paul Kane. For two and a half years he traveled in Canada, sketching Indian life to illustrate a book that he wrote, *Wanderings of an Artist Among the Indians*.

Below is a view of an Indian camp on the Columbia River, near the Pacific Coast. The tall lodges are made of mats stretched over poles. Salmon, which are plentiful in the region, are hung on horizontal poles to dry.

Indian Camp Colville, after 1847, oil, Royal Ontario Museum, Toronto

The Jolly Flatboatmen in Port,
detail, 1857, oil,
City Art Museum of St. Louis

George Caleb Bingham, who lived in Missouri, painted scenes of life along the Mississippi and Missouri rivers. He made countless sketches of people in various poses and used them to compose large oil paintings.

At left is a scene of boatmen on the Mississippi. It shows people who work on the river enjoying themselves along the waterfront. There is a great sense of joyfulness in the painting. The difference between the figures in motion and those at rest is striking. Many copies of Bingham's river paintings were printed and became popular throughout the country.

About 1850, pencil and wash,
Museum of Fine Arts, Boston,
M. and M. Karolik Collection

TAYLOR HICKS

Fur Traders Descending the Missouri,
1845, oil, The Metropolitan Museum
of Art, Morris K. Jesup Fund, 1933

The Missouri River was a main route for fur trappers and traders. Bingham's painting above shows a French fur trader paddling down the river in a dugout canoe. Leaning lazily on the cargo of furs is his son. A captive fox sits chained in the bow. The artist has caught the feeling of immense quiet in the morning mist and in the glassy reflections on the water.

When gold was discovered in California an artist, Charles Nahl, joined the gold rush. Nahl worked in the mines and painted the rough mining camp life. In the Sunday scene below he shows various activities of miners on their day off.

Sunday Morning in the Mines, detail, 1872, oil, E. B. Crocker Art Gallery

1869, oil, The Butler Institute of American Art

Spectacular landscapes of the West were painted on huge canvases by Albert Bierstadt. He was a member of an expedition that traveled the Oregon Trail, which started in Missouri and ran over plains and mountains to the Columbia River in the Pacific Northwest. This trail had been used by fur traders for many years and had become a popular route for pioneer families heading west.

When Bierstadt traveled this rugged route he made many sketches of the landscape and of the early travelers with their covered wagons. In his painting, *The Oregon Trail,* at left, the sky and mountains seem to go on forever. Each figure in the foreground is painted with great care, even the grazing cattle and sheep. The tiny figures in the distance emphasize the large scale of the mountains.

The landscape below is by Thomas Moran, the official artist for an expedition that explored the canyon of the Yellowstone River. This watercolor painting is a view of the Great Blue Spring of the Lower Geyser Basin. Moran's paintings of the Grand Canyon of the Yellowstone helped to persuade Congress to establish the Yellowstone area as America's first national park.

1871, Hirschl and Adler Galleries

On Toward Nauvoo, 1880's, oil, Art Collection, Brigham Young University

The largest organized migration in the history of the American West was that of the Mormons, members of the Church of Jesus Christ of Latter-Day Saints. From the time their church was founded the Mormons were persecuted by unfriendly neighbors, and forced to move on from New York, Ohio, Missouri and Illinois. Finally they settled in the Great Salt Lake Basin in Utah.

The story of the first years of the Mormon church was painted by Carl C. A. Christensen in twenty-two scenes on a canvas roll which stretched 175 feet. The long canvas was unrolled as the artist gave lectures describing each scene. Above, Mormon families are preparing to leave Missouri in covered wagons.

1889, oil, Amon Carter Museum, Forth Worth, Texas

The best-known artist of the West was Frederic Remington. He was born in New York State, the son of a Civil War cavalry officer. Remington studied art for a year at Yale, where he was also a boxer and a football player. Then he went west, working as a cowboy and prospecting for gold in Arizona. He roamed on cattle trails from Canada to the Mexican border, and became an expert in handling a lariat and a six-gun.

Remington captured on canvas the disappearing world of the cowboy
and the Army cavalryman. In *A Dash for Timber*, he shows American troopers
retreating from a war party of Indians.

The colorful mountain men whose era was already past interested Remington.
He made this quick sketch and called it *The French Trapper*. The positions
of the central figure and the distant pack animals were changed for the
finished oil painting, which he called *The Half-Breed Trapper*.

1889, pen and ink, Remington
Art Museum, Ogdensburg, New York

1889, Amon Carter Museum

The Sentinel, 1907, oil, Remington Art Museum

Remington's paintings reflected the hardships of the Old West, where settlers fought to establish new homes while Indians tried to protect their lands. Even his quiet scenes are filled with a sense of danger. Above, a grizzled pioneer stands in the moonlight with his rifle ready, guarding a sleeping wagon train. The lone, upright figure and the large round wheels on either side create a strong design.

The Indian scout in the empty night scene below seems alert to possible danger. He has just halted his horse and now leans forward to sense whether the people in the distance are friends or enemies.

Remington first became well known as a magazine illustrator. As time went on he wrote his own articles and books on Western subjects. In later years he devoted himself to oil painting.

The Scout: Friends or Enemies, detail, about 1890, oil, Sterling and Francine Clark Art Institute, Williamstown, Massachusetts

From his childhood Remington loved horses, and he became a master at portraying them in motion. He made endless sketches of horses galloping, jumping, rearing and bucking. Earlier artists were not really aware of the position of horses' legs in rapid motion. But the development, in Remington's time, of fast-action photography revealed exactly how a running horse's legs move.

Cowboy Camp During the Roundup, detail, about 1887, oil, Amon Carter Museum

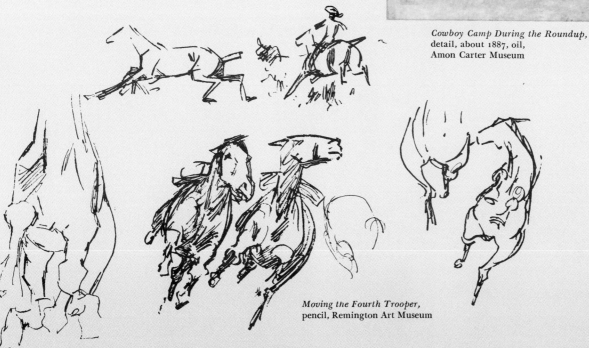

Moving the Fourth Trooper, pencil, Remington Art Museum

Charles Marion Russell, sometimes called "Kid" Russell, became known as the "cowboy artist." Born in St. Louis, he went to Montana at sixteen, where he worked as a sheepherder, horse wrangler and cowhand.

Russell loved the open ranges, the Indian ways, the great sky, the wild life and the freedom of the West. In this scene cowboys are preparing for spring round-up, when they gather the cattle which have wintered on the open range. The men are breaking in wild horses.

The Wild Horse Hunters, 1913,
oil, Amon Carter Museum

Russell understood a cowboy's life. He knew its romance, adventure and

back-breaking work. He had taken part in wild horse hunts. Here he shows a

stampeding horse trapped in a cowboy's lasso while others scramble wildly to escape.

"Kid" Russell enjoyed the roughhousing of cowboys at play. He showed his boisterous friends riding into town, their guns blazing. This rowdy scene of cowboys crashing into a hotel and gambling casino is titled *In Without Knocking*. The drawing of the cow's skull near Russell's signature became a kind of trademark on his paintings.

1909, oil, Amon Carter Museum

Sculpture of the Old West ranges from reliefs on small coins to larger-than-life-sized monuments in parks and other public places.

The painter Frederic Remington turned to sculpture late in his life. He made small statues in order to give fuller expression to action than was possible on a flat surface. In *Bronco Buster* there is a wonderful sense of movement and balance.

About 1905,
The Metropolitan Museum of Art,
Bequest of Jacob Ruppert, 1939

A leading American sculptor, James Earle Fraser, who was brought up in South Dakota, designed the famous five-cent coin known as the "Buffalo Nickel." Three different Indians posed for the profile head.

Cyrus Dallin, born in Utah of pioneer parents, was one of the first American artists to come from the West. He was studying art in Paris when "Buffalo Bill" Cody's Wild West Show played there. The performances of the cowboys and Indians probably inspired him to use Indian themes in sculpture. His statue *The Appeal to the Great Spirit* stands in front of the Museum of Fine Arts in Boston.

1909, Museum of Fine Arts, Boston, Gift of Peter C. Brooks and Others

1888, oil,
Philadelphia
Museum of Art,
Given by Mrs.
Thomas Eakins
and Miss
Mary A. Williams

Thomas Eakins, one of America's most important artists, spent some time on a ranch in North Dakota, living with cowboys, wearing their clothes and joining in their fun. Back home again in Philadelphia, he posed his friends in Western clothes, complete with spurs and guns. In *Home Ranch,* at left, one of Eakins' friends sits cross-legged in the center of the painting, singing and playing the guitar. The man seated at the table is watching the singer and seems to be listening intently.

1889, The Metropolitan Museum of Art, Museum Accession 1961

The black cat and the objects strewn on the floor give the painting a homey feeling.

Eakins was one of the first important artists to use photography as a part of his work. He experimented with photographs of people in action in order to study their movements. He often used his photographs as material for his paintings. The Eakins photograph above, of a seated cowboy, was taken during his Western trip. Eakins' camera portraits are works of art in themselves.

1875, National Archives

An early use of photography in the West was to take pictures of trails, valleys and mountain passes, in order to plot routes for wagon roads and railways. Photography also was used to survey the topography of the West, locate mineral deposits and record the life of the Indians.

William Henry Jackson was a photographer who traveled back and forth across the West, first on wagon trains, then on the new railroads. He photographed miners in their camps and railroad workers laying tracks. Above is a Jackson photograph of prospectors camping out near their mine in Colorado.

1869, Union Pacific Railroad Photo

This photograph by Jackson shows a train crossing a wooden trestle.

Jackson's photographs of Yellowstone, in addition to the paintings by Thomas

Moran, helped convince the country that this scenic wonder should be preserved.

About 1875, Collection of Weston J. Naef

ack Hillers was the photographer for an expedition that explored the Grand Canyon region in Arizona. He took pictures of this spectacular scenery and of Indians in their homes. Above is a Hillers photograph of Hopi Indians posed in front of their pueblos in Wolpi, Arizona.

In the early days of photography cameras were big and bulky. Picture-taking was a slow process. The fastest exposures might last as long as fifteen seconds. In spite of these difficulties early Western photographers made magnificent pictures of people and scenery.

The official photographer for several government expeditions to the West was Timothy O'Sullivan. He photographed mountains, canyons, rivers and lakes, as well as Indians.

At left is an O'Sullivan photograph of Canyon de Chelly, Arizona. Tucked into a natural cavity in the rock cliff are ruins of an ancient Pueblo Indian dwelling. The photographer was able to capture the quality of the texture of the rock.

1873, Denver Public
Library Western Collection

1873, Library of Congress

O'Sullivan photographed this Zuñi war chief, at left, dressed in a fine blanket and silver necklace.

One of the best-known photographers of the Indians was Edward Curtis. He traveled thousands of miles to take pictures of Indians. With his clumsy camera he photographed eighty Western tribes. Below, left, is a Curtis photograph of a Quilcène boy who lived in what is now the state of Washington. Below, right, is a Navajo of New Mexico, dressed for a religious dance.

1904, Library of Congress

1912, Denver Public Library
Western Collection

This photograph of early days in Colorado shows a mining town in the Rocky Mountains. A pack train has come to a halt in the unpaved streets. The man posed leaning on his bicycle adds variety to the picture. The photograph shows Colorado

About 1887, Library, State Historical Society of Colorado

architecture of the period. False fronts were added to plain barnlike buildings to make them look more elegant. The evergreen trees surrounded by snow on the steep mountain slope make an interesting backdrop to the scene.

Cow's Skull: Red, White and Blue, 193
oil, The Metropolitan Museum of Ar
The Alfred Stieglitz Collection, 19

Early twentieth
century, oil,
Phoenix Art Museum

arly in the twentieth century a group of Eastern painters settled in northern

New Mexico, and made it into one of the great art centers of the world. These

modern artists found beauty in the colors, shapes and patterns of the Southwestern

mountains and deserts.

The painting above of an Indian girl from the Santa Clara Pueblo is by

Robert Henri, who was inspired by Western themes.

Georgia O'Keeffe paints the stark shapes of simple things: dead leaves, stones,

desert flowers, weathered wood and bleached animal bones.

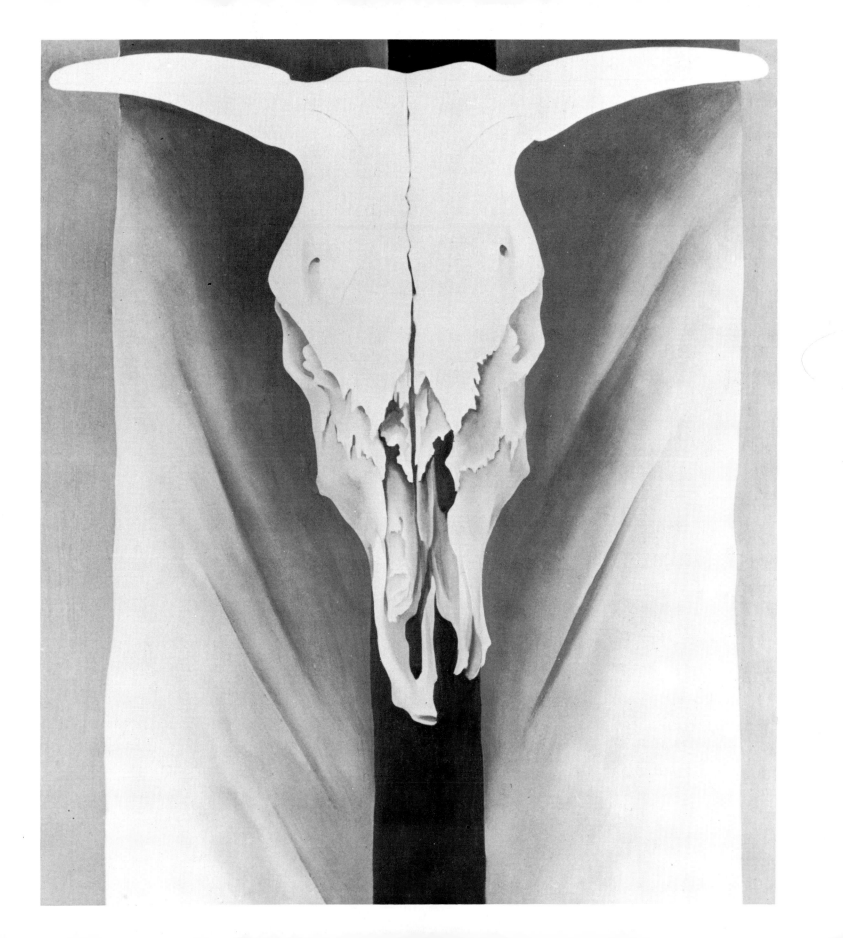

What is known as the Old West lasted for little more than a hundred years. In that short time the herds of buffalo and the unfenced cattle ranges vanished forever. The rough-riding cavalrymen, the sun-hardened cowboys, the pioneers and the grizzled prospectors have disappeared. The earliest inhabitants—the Indian tribes of the Great Plains, the Southwest and the Pacific Coast—no longer roam the land. But the Old West lives on in the paintings, sculptures and photographs of the pioneer artists who have preserved its memory.

Medicine Arrow,
by E. Irving Couse,
early twentieth century, oil,
Hirschl and Adler Galleries